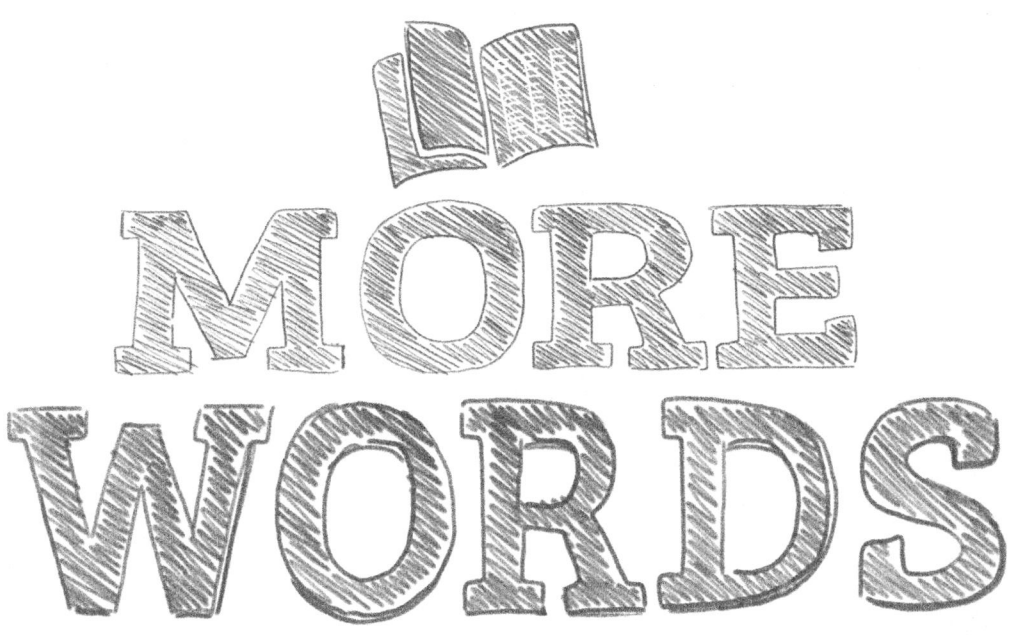

By Pam Mehlin

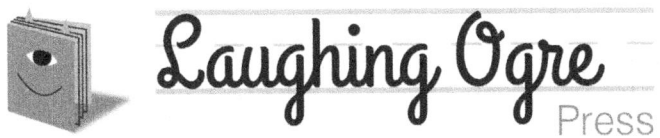

© 2019 Laughing Ogre Press®. All rights reserved.

Acknowledgments

I would like to thank Karen Sonday and Tracie Ditty for their unyielding support and guidance through the years as I voraciously compiled word lists. In addition, thanks to Arlene Sonday who provided a platform/base with the Sonday System reading and spelling curriculum. I will be forever appreciative to Karen and Arlene for their mentoring and wisdom. Lastly, thank you to Monette Kollodge who patiently formatted, reformatted and supported me throughout this process.

© 2019 Laughing Ogre Press®. All rights reserved.

No part of this book may be reproduced, re-sold, or utilized in any form or by any electronic or mechanical means, including photocopying, without permission in writing from the publisher.

Laughing Ogre Press®
www.laughingogrepress.com

Ordering Information:

Quantity sales: Special discounts are available on quantity purchases by corporations, associations, and others. For details, contact the publisher.

Orders by U.S: trade bookstores and wholesalers. Please contact Laughing Ogre Press: www.laughingogrepress.com.

Printed in the United States of America

First Printing, 2019

ISBN 978-0-9989181-4-3

Table of Contents

/ă/ layered lists 2
/ĭ/ layered lists 3
/ŏ/ layered lists 4
/ŭ/ layered lists 5
/ĕ/ layered lists 6
tw-, **dw-** and **sk-** 7
-pt, **-tz** 8
nonsense words 9
-x 10
ay in the middle of a word 11
ee at the end of a word 12
oy in the middle of the word 13
oo at the end of a word 14
oo in multisyllabic words 15
final **y** /ī/ in multisyllabic words 16
closed syllables 17
open syllables 18
v/cv, **vc/v** open and closed 19
y /ī/ in closed syllables 20
y /ī/ in open syllables 21
vce syllables 22
vc/ccv and **vcc/cv** 23
a-e open, closed, **vce** 24
i-e open, closed, **vce** 25
-ire, **-ile** 26
o-e open, closed, **vce** 27
u-e /oo/ open, closed, **vce** 28
u-e /ū/ open, closed, **vce** 29
e-e open, closed, **vce** 30
y-e /ī/ 31
-vre 32
final /**v**/ in silent **e** words 33
s as /**z**/ in silent **e** words 34
s as /**s**/ in silent **e** words 35
other forms of silent **e** 36
words ending in **-f** to **-ves** 37
r controlled syllables 38
r controlled **y** 39
vowel pairs 40
-cle syllables 41
-cle nonsense words 42
wh /**w**/ and **wh** /**h**/ 43
er not a suffix 44
ow not followed by **n** or **l** 45
ow multisyllabic words 46
/**ch**/ in multisyllabic words 47
-age /ij/ 48
-age /äzh/ 49
-dge multisyllabic words 50
-ange 51
soft **g** exceptions 52
/j/ after a short vowel not **-dge** 53
cent 55
cide, **cid**, **cise** families 56
ke/**ki** 57
-ed /ed/ /id/ 58
-ed /d/ 59
-ed /t/ 60
mixed **-ed** 61
-ct /kt/ and **-cked** 62
/st/ and /nd/ 63
words ending in **-id** 64
a /ə/ at the end of the word 65
a /ə/ at the end of multisyllabic words 66
ai before **n** or **l** 67
ir /ər/ 68
ai not before **n**, **l** 69
air words 70
ai 71
v/v 72
v/v, **i** /ē/ 73
long vowel in closed syllables 74
ur 75
-tion 76
multisyllabic **-tion** 77
-fle and **-ful** 78
-ckle, **-ickle**, **icle** and **ical** /ikal/ 79
-ic 80
-ic plus **e**, **i**, **y** suffixes 81
doubling rule 82
-ous, **-us**, **-ess** words 83
-al plus **-ly** 84
-tle and **-tal** 85
words ending in **-el** /əl/ 86
ation / **ative** / **able** 87
-ish 88
elision and **contractions** 89
e rule dropping the **e** 90
e rule keep the **e** 91
e rule exceptions 92
doubling /**e** rule pairs 93
-cle plus **-y** 94
multisyllabic **au** /o̊/ 95
sion /shən/ 96
roots ending in **-ss** 97
roots ending in **-ss** 98
roots ending in **-ss** 99
/shən/, /zhən/ exceptions 100
y rule, change the **y** to **i** 101
y rule don't change the **y** to **i** with **i** suffixes 102
y rule don't change the **y** to **i** with vowel pairs 103
y rule when adding **s**, change the **y** to **i** add **es** 104
mixed endings rules 105
ie 106
ei 107
g not silent 108
-gn 109
cu /ku/ 110
tu /choo/ 111
du /joo/ 112
su, **sure** 113
days of the week and months of the year 114
number words 115
-logy/**-logist** 116
mixed **-ct** roots 117
y as /ī/ with all syllable types 118
/y/ after **n** or **l** 119
i /ē/ 120
i /ē/ 121
i /ē/ 122
i /ē/ 123
-ity 124
-ine 125
ci /sh/ 126
ci /sh/ 127
ci /sh/ 128
s, **ch**, **sch** /sh/ 129
ti /sh/ 130
ti /sh/ 131

/ă/ layered lists

cvc	blends	some /ə/
nap	stand	knapsack
bag	cramp	gallant
cab	grant	stagnant
zap	smash	tangram
man	snack	transplant
ram	blanch	ransack
sag	draft	bantam
cat	grasp	canvas
lab	scamp	rampant
gap	plant	banana
dab	gland	anthrax
fan	slant	phantasm
jag	tract	valance
Pam	branch	madam
fad	stamp	canal
nab	snack	balance
hag	swam	bandana
pal	gramp	rascal
ham	bland	vandal
lap	flask	anagram
rat	quack	cabana
zag	craft	granddad
bat	clamp	scalawag

/ɪ/ layered lists

cvc	blends	some /ə/
kid	skimp	lipstick
hip	twist	distilling
fit	flint	picnic
bib	stint	nitpick
dig	blimp	midriff
him	glint	implicit
jig	crimp	inflict
kin	drift	shindig
lid	primp	vindictive
Tim	grist	discipline
nip	swift	indivisible
pit	crisp	infinite
rim	brisk	liquid
Sid	print	dismissing
bit	swish	finishing
win	clinch	impinge
fix	quint	diminish
yip	plink	gimmick
Liz	swill	infringing
did	twitch	inhibitive
fig	fling	dismissive
mid	film	inquisitive
zip	skit	intrinsic
tin	kiln	indistinct
rib	frisk	pilgrim

/ŏ/ layered lists

cvc	blends	some /ə/
Bob	slosh	concoct
not	chomp	pompom
cop	sloth	bonbon
dog	frond	hobnob
mod	blotch	hotdog
lot	stock	blossom
fob	tromp	throttle
rot	Scott	dollop
pop	blond	bottom
dot	floss	cotton
fog	plop	common
gob	doll	oblong
hot	stomp	nonstop
jog	broth	Boston
lop	frost	wonton
cod	loft	monolog
bog	clomp	poptop
nod	scotch	hopscotch
mop	cloth	
rob	cross	
tot		
sob		
pot		
fog		

/ŭ/ layered lists

cvc	blends	with /ə/
bug	stump	fungus
nut	crunch	subgum
pup	grunt	hubbub
gut	frump	sunup
lug	crust	rumpus
pun	stunk	unjust
cut	brunt	yumyum
rug	brunch	succumb
tux	plump	humdrum
yum	trust	unplugs
pug	clutch	numskull
run	slush	dumdum
hut	blunt	cupful
dug	trump	uncut
hum	crush	humbug
jug	clung	unstuck
bun	crutch	hummus
mug	plunk	subcult
but	skulk	upchuck
sum	shunt	untuck
cup	thump	buzzcut
fun	grump	
bum	skunk	
sun	flush	
rut	chump	
	brush	

/ĕ/ layered lists

cvc	blends	some /ə/
Ken	blend	velvet
red	spent	extent
met	melt	element
led	stench	tempest
ten	press	excess
fed	etch	crescent
men	vest	vestment
bed	length	empress
hen	cleft	helmet
net	smelt	excellent
wed	elk	strengthen
beg	theft	fennel
pen	desk	pellet
bet	temp	segment
web	drench	kennel
leg	bless	emblem
den	chest	vestment
peg	spend	expel
get	trend	legend
keg		
let		
hem		
jet		

tw-, dw- and sk-

twig	tweezers	skate
two	twentieth	skill
'twas	between	skit
twist	entwine	sky
tweed	twelve	skid
twill	twelfth	skim
twit	twenty	skin
twixt	twinkle	skip
tweet	twinge	ski
twin	twilight	skimp
twist	twitter	skiff
twang		skill
twine	dwell	skirt
twirl	dwarf	skivvies
twice	dwarves	skiffle
twerp	dweeb	skirmish
tweak	dwelt	skitter
twirp	dwindle	skiddoo
tweens		skillet
twitch	skull	skittle
Twinkies	skunk	skinny
twister	skulk	skipper

-pt, -tz

apt	exempt	blitz
opt	abrupt	spritz
sept	accept	quartz
clept	adapt	fritz
kept	adept	glitz
wept	adopt	klutz
rapt	inept	chintz
kempt	erupt	ditz
tempt	excerpt	putz
slept	attempt	ritz
prompt	bankrupt	waltz
crypt	preempt	
leapt	disrupt	
crept	except	
swept	unkempt	
sculpt		
script		

nonsense words

slox	clant	stinth
blemp	smond	blach
spant	shaff	crump
grund	chemp	cleeg
chack	glizz	brund
sliff	swust	frelt
plick	frift	flist
swenth	drelk	drask
flist	chosh	grosh
sheeb	geesh	crift
gluft	slect	broff
frilt	wezz	proth
chib	plust	plish
flesp	quep	sloct
scush	scoth	breesh
stask	bresh	cront
froch	grelt	glast
trisp	smeech	blesh
zoll	crolt	trusp
bruct	shimp	chith
slux	sizz	froff
stost	frand	glend

-x

ax	fox	borax	Kleenex
ex	lox	FedEx	spandex
ox	mix	helix	convex
box	pix	index	climax
fax	tax	latex	sphinx
lax	plex	remix	vertex
nix	flax	unfix	larynx
pox	minx	detox	matrix
tux	crux	phlox	thorax
wax	flex	relax	cortex
fix	jinx	Pyrex	apex
hex	flux	reflex	Phoenix
lex	coax	suffix	equinox
max	hoax	prefix	anthrax
sax	onyx	affix	appendix
pax	oryx	conflux	orthodox
vex	lynx	perplex	multiplex
dex	annex	simplex	

ay in the middle of a word

ay /ā/

mayo

layer

crayon

Crayola

naysayer

bayonet

mayor

layette

rayon

kayo

mayhem

mayonnaise

ay /ī/

kayak

Mayan

papaya

piraya

cayenne

ee at the end of a word

bee	designee	manatee
fee	yippee	settee
gee	whoopee	emcee
wee	toffee	amputee
Dee	teepee	devotee
Lee	bungee	honoree
see	coffee	nominee
tee	chickadee	refugee
flee	frisbee	trustee
free	freebee	employee
whee	jubilee	invitee
knee	bumblebee	licensee
tree	guarantee	enrollee
glee	fricassee	consignee
thee	filigree	deportee
three	dungaree	detainee
spree	pedigree	trainee
agree	honeybee	retiree
decree	carefree	referee
degree	squeegee	committee
	jamboree	sponsee

oy in the middle of the word

foyer

loyal

royal

oyster

voyage

buoyant

benzoyl

boycott

gargoyle

flamboyant

clairvoyant

boysenberry

oo at the end of a word

boo	yahoo
too	taboo
zoo	igloo
goo	kazoo
moo	voodoo
woo	tattoo
shoo	skidoo
coo	buckaroo
loo	peekaboo
	bamboo
	cuckoo
	hoodoo
	bugaboo
	shampoo
	cockatoo
	cockapoo
	kangaroo
	buckeroo
	switcheroo
	choochoo
	achoo
	googoo
	hallaballoo

oo in multisyllabic words

aloof	baboon	wooden
varoom	bassoon	booger
tycoon	cocoon	woolen
oodles	raccoon	cookies
noodle	papoose	plywood
loosen	platoon	boogeyman
groovy	saloon	hooray
lagoon	maroon	booboo
voodoo	lampoon	phooey
hoodoo	chinook	tomfoolery
poodle	balloon	vamoose
buffoon	cartoon	whoopee
cahoots	cooper	bazooka
doodle	blooper	boondocks
whoopee	monsoon	macaroon
festoon	harpoon	bamboozle
coolant	typhoon	boomerangs
pontoon	dragoon	hoodwinked
kazoos	doodad	nincompoop
hoodlum	poodle	pantaloon
oompah	buffoon	boondoggle
tycoon	tootsie	doomsdayer
blooper	behoove	kookaburra

final **y** /ī/ in multisyllabic words

	-ify
apply	pacify
defy	dignify
rely	certify
deny	gratify
reply	clarify
imply	fortify
supply	horrify
comply	petrify
July	signify
multiply	classify
satisfy	mortify
occupy	testify
refry	intensify
retry	rectify
reapply	falsify
	codify
	unify

closed syllables

closed syllables	vc/cv	
fom	mag/net	plas/tic
pik	goblet	muffin
jun	sandal	segment
beb	convent	velvet
haz	syntax	dentist
ic	ransom	bandit
yex	signet	husband
wiv	tendril	picnic
quif	cosmic	canyon
av	falcon	walnut
dop	until	tablet
min	cactus	campus
hus	plastic	problem
ex	mascot	pretzel
lud	seldom	goblin
mep	helmet	trumpet
sim	napkin	nutmeg
ket	wisdom	album
jos	solvent	mantis
zat	tonsil	tinsel
	witness	shindig
	tidbit	mustang
	trespass	figment

open syllables

open syllables	2 syllables		y as /ē/
mo	bo/lo	po/lo	po/ny
li	ego	yoyo	navy
ke	deny	rely	gravy
bu	halo	tofu	puny
vy	zero	juju	ivy
co	solo	mojo	baby
se	tutu	hypo	holy
za	veto	gogo	lady
wi	Fido	hobo	ruby
de	logo	typo	crazy
fu	judo	defy	tidy
hy	silo	boho	duty
tu	promo	repo	lazy
pa	July	pogo	zany
jy	Lulu	dodo	Cody
	moto	nono	hazy
		Coco	phony
			holy moly

v/cv, vc/v open and closed

habit	human
melon	legal
moment	comet
chosen	camel
student	rapid
beyond	visit
robin	wagon
limit	seven
level	novel
vanish	credit
open	robot
even	bonus
bacon	tulip
planet	rodent
finish	sequel
closet	cabin
haven	begin
rapid	tiger
focus	motel
belong	bogus
demon	nomad
crocus	cupid
lemon	linen
nylon	began
raven	frozen

y /ĭ/ in closed syllables

myth	Egypt	mystical
hymn	cygnet	typical
nymph	symptom	symphony
lynch	crystal	sympathy
lynx	gypsy	oxygen
crypt	gypsum	synthetic
sylph	rhythmic	symmetry
styx	syntax	homonym
tryst	cynic	photosynthesis
lymph	typical	analysis
sync	cynical	Olympics
synch	abyss	synopsis
gym	Phyllis	antonym
	hymnal	calypso
	symbol	abysmal
	polyps	eucalyptus
	gymnast	acrylic
	synonym	mythological

y /ī/ in open syllables

stylist
pylon
typist
gyrate
cyclone
cyclops
hydrant
cypress
tycoon
tyrant
stylus
typhoon
hyphen
python
pyrite
hybrid
hygiene
supply
unicycle
myopic

dynamic
hyacinth
cyanide
pyromaniac
hydroponic
gyroscope
dynamo
dynamite
hydroplane
hydrogen
myopic
xylophone
hydraulic
cyber
hydroxide

vce syllables

vce	flute	grove
ine	crane	shine
efe	choke	grade
uke	drove	Steve
ope	flake	slime
ase	chime	smile
yte	prune	Eve
ade	style	dude
eze	blade	grate
ile	hole	scope
ome	graze	throne
une	crime	chafe
ybe	slope	meme
ete	duke	slate
ule	type	hype
ise	shame	Pete
ove	tribe	fluke
ake	shone	snake
yve	flute	bile
ipe	these	prone
oke	vase	flame
ese		

vc/ccv and **vcc/cv**

pumpkin
membrane
spectrum
mandrill
pilgrim
hundred
children
sandwich
brethren
ostrich
English
nostril
tendril
ringlet
tantrum
dandruff
bumpkin
hipster
tangram

menthol
dolphin
monster
simply
culprit
antler
simplex

a-e open, closed, vce

evade	butane	promenade
estate	pomade	microscale
concave	profane	regulate
donate	escape	captivate
crusade	decade	stimulate
vibrate	erase	calculate
membrane	stockade	renovate
tirade	debate	escalate
encase	propane	elevate
equate	fixate	regale
defame	mundane	resale
impale	rebate	marinade
prebake	female	tapenade
exhale	mistake	elongate
primate	relate	contemplate
enflame	awake	generate
octane	pinwale	decapitate
unsafe	folktale	
behave	emblaze	
humane	sulfate	
methane	migrate	

i-e open, closed, **vce**

describe	pinstripe
textile	senile
profile	precise
revise	baptize
tactile	transcribe
subscribe	frostbite
hitchhike	yuletide
revive	confine
polite	endive
capsize	reptile
reside	sublime
compile	diatribe
provide	insecticide
bromide	alkaline
advise	crocodile
awhile	hydroxide
midlife	satellite
recline	infantile
dislike	pantomime
entwine	dioxide

-ire, -ile

inquire	agile
rewire	guile
umpire	profile
desire	awhile
entire	compile
bonfire	exile
vampire	senile
require	gentile
haywire	juvenile
campfire	reptile
perspire	sandpile
hardwire	profile
backfire	textile
tightwire	projectile
quagmire	crocodile
esquire	percentile
gunfire	worthwhile
barbwire	infantile
conspire	reconcile
retire	turnstile
inspire	bibliophile

o-e open, closed, **vce**

erode	antelope
glucose	microbe
encode	provolone
ozone	episode
implode	silicone
propose	isotope
upstroke	envelope
elope	microscope
revoke	bellicose
tadpole	juxtapose
cyclone	repose
enclose	explode
lactose	invoke
trombone	provoke
fructose	decode
dextrose	expose
emote	impose
alcove	suppose
devote	comatose
rewove	dictaphone

u-e /oo/ open, closed, **vce**

dilute	minute	absolute
resume	include	altitude
multitude	exclude	constitute
intrude	elude	fortitude
protrude	obtuse	institute
salute	legume	longitude
exude	presume	gratitude
reduce	astute	substitute
resume		magnitude
pollute		resolute
costume		latitude
consume		
delude		
prelude		
solitude		
attitude		
exhume		
collude		

u-e /ū/ open, closed, **vce**

rebuke	minuscule
granule	vestibule
globule	distribute
abuse	electrocute
tribune	ridicule
amuse	molecule
dispute	compute
accuse	refute
excuse	infuse
immune	diffuse
refuse	defuse
volume	perfume
confuse	repute
execute	acute
tribute	disrepute

e-e open, closed, **vce**

trapeze
complete
delete
athlete
convene
stampede
concrete
extreme
compete
deplete
impede
gangrene
excrete
obscene
concede
accede
benzene
secede
obsolete
discrete
replete
intervene

y-e /ī/

style	analyze	**-yre**
Clyde	paralyze	pyre
tyne	hairstyle	lyre
thyme	freestyle	byre
Lyle	subtype	gyre
hype	enzyme	
type	anodyne	
byte	electrolyze	
megabyte	rhyme	
argyle	lyrist	

-vre

-are	-ere	-ire	-ore
Medicare	cohere	empire	explore
ovenware	adhere	retire	before
hardware	revere	expire	adore
non-glare	sincere	inspire	implore
welfare	severe	admire	ignore
anti-glare	cashmere	attire	galore
aware	belvedere	rehire	restore
ensnare	atmosphere	satire	anymore
compare	hemisphere	perspire	deplore
daycare	premiere	quagmire	folklore
glassware		entire	drugstore
declare		conspire	sophomore
prepare		require	Singapore
fanfare			albacore
software			hardcore
spyware			pinafore
malware			sycamore
			commodore
			offshore

final /v/ in silent e words

long vowel		short vowel -lve	vowel pairs	r control
eve	stove	delve	mauve	carve
cave	drove	calve	waive	nerve
hove	grove	halve	weave	serve
pave	trove	salve	heave	curve
save	clove	valve	leave	starve
wove	knave	solve	sieve	swerve
cove	brave	twelve	peeve	
fave	chive	shelve	grieve	
jive	drive	evolve	cleave	
rave	grave		groove	
dive	shave	prove*	thieve	
five	strive	move*	sleeve	
nave	thrive	glove*	believe	
wave		shove*	achieve	
dove	**short**	love*	receive	
gave	**vowel**	above*	perceive	
hive	give	dove*	deceive	
live	have		conceive	
rove	live			
	olive			

*/oo/ and /ə/

s as /z/ in **silent e** words

tease	these	televise
lose	arouse	exorcise
braise	amuse	propose
praise	refuse	primrose
cause	compose	transpose
clause	repose	because
whose	excuse	decompose
phase	infuse	chastise
phrase	abuse	confuse
choose	disguise	enterprise
please	surmise	circumfuse
cheese	revise	archdiocese
noise	advise	comprise
cleanse	accuse	compromise
browse	appraise	supervise
bruise	devise	improvise
poise	despise	demise
cruise	appease	
pause	applause	
raise	suppose	
rouse	exercise	
those	disease	

s as /s/ in **silent e** words

else	horse	immense
chase	worse	incense
dowse	verse	intense
sense	nurse	license
dense	purse	elapse
cense	curse	eclipse
false	parse	impulse
pulse	hearse	condense
tense	hoarse	diagnose
geese	crease	lacrosse
grease	spouse	traverse
cease	purpose	universe
hoarse	pretense	bellicose
house	recourse	caboose
mouse	excuse	reimburse
blouse	refuse	concise
loose	diffuse	precise
goose	abuse	decease
moose	offense	decrease
lease	dispense	increase
course	suspense	reverse
grouse	endorse	converse
mousse	defense	inverse
coarse		

other forms of **silent e**

-aste long a	-the /th/	-pse
baste	soothe	lapse
haste	swathe	corpse
taste	lathe	glimpse
waste	breathe	relapse
paste	bathe	collapse
chaste	loathe	traipse
toothpaste	teethe	eclipse
posthaste	writhe	apocalypse
aftertaste	lithe	synapse
	scythe	copse
	clothe	elapse
	scathe	ellipse
	tithe	prolapse
	blithe	
	seethe	

words ending in **-f** to **-ves**

wife →	wives
wolf	wolves
life	lives
calf	calves
knife	knives
elf	elves
half	halves
self	selves
shelf	shelves
wharf	wharves
wolf	wolves
leaf	leaves
scarf	scarves
loaf	loaves
thief	thieves
belief	believes
relief	relieves
grief	grieves

r controlled syllables

r controlled syllables

	par/take	dir/ect
dar	corner	journal
ter	whimper	mourning
gor	plaster	turbine
jer	cargo	dairy
har	garden	sojourn
ker	garter	despair
teer	butler	mooring
lar	hornet	weird
mor	orbit	surely
zer	vortex	learner
	pardon	pier
dir	carbon	premiere
mier	lantern	earthling
nur	swelter	heiress
mour	whisper	airplane
cair	termite	burden
toor	forlorn	converge
lear	vermin	collar
zeir	torment	professor

r controlled **y**

yr /er/	**yr /ear/**
satyr	lyric
syrup	lyrical
myrrh	lyricist
martyr	pyramid
Myrtle	myriad
zephyr	tyranny
syringe	Pyrenees
labyrinth	
tyrannosaurus	

vowel pairs

vowel pair syllables

yeep	mon/soon	re/main/der
moin	deltoid	bleachers
zoop	maroon	toenail
nay	tweezer	achieve
zow	convoy	cashew
poy	delay	fruit juice
	sixteen	dawning
bain	rooster	jersey
weab	Friday	laundered
foun	chowder	ceiling
niet	ointment	sealing
tew	window	dewdrop
baw	deploy	Kelsey
jey	tabloid	receipt
cein	canteen	heather
daut	harpoon	explain
hoab	okay	compound
gue	boycott	withdrawn
buim	esteem	daunting
goe	portray	brownie
	flower	snowboarder
	poison	values

-cle syllables

-cle

-ble	re/sem/ble	mi/cro/par/ti/cle
-cle	popsicle	obstacle
-ckle	cubicle	multiple
-kle	pineapple	soluble
-dle	follicle	example
-fle	ramshackle	pinnacle
-ple	bicycle	caboodle
-stle	tentacle	quadruple
-tle	skedaddle	spectacle
-zle	principle	finagle
	disgruntled	tabernacle
	corpuscle	participle
	rectangle	bamboozle
	cuticle	octangle
	bedazzle	disciple
	boondoggle	oracle
	icicle	receptacle
	centuple	clavicle

-cle nonsense words

imble	mapple	befle
fleckle	lergle	bogle
dadle	kyzle	torple
puffle	hintle	pertle
argle	kimble	hifle
hipple	jacle	spinkle
bitle	addle	lozle
vuzzle	logle	wygle
orkle	pepple	bemble
bebble	tytle	motle
pocle	rezzle	nifle
sattle	wackle	vezzle
rizle	quible	cudle
junkle	tarcle	jinkle
fandle	dadle	gopple

wh /w/ and wh /h/

/w/		/h/
whatever	whirlwind	who
whatnots	whitecaps	whom
wheeze	everywhere	whose
wherever	pinwheel	whole
whiffle	overwhelms	whodunnit
whimper	whatsoever	wholesale
whisker	whereabouts	wholesome
whistle	wherefore	whosoever
whisper	whiplash	wholeheartedly
whiplash	whirlpools	
whiten	worthwhile	
whoopee	cartwheels	
bushwhack	wheelchair	
freewheel	wherewithal	
meanwhile	whichsoever	
somewhat	whimsical	
whalebone	whatchamacallit	
whereupon	wherewithin	
whichever		

er not a suffix

her	merge	gerbil	geranium
jerk	serge	desert	cerebral
over	berth	dessert	moderate
ever	clerk	divert	intercom
pert		alert	generate
berg		anger	emerald
erst		mercy	average
herb		derby	lateral
perk		excerpt	inferno
therm		sliver	ceramic
verb		silver	celery
herd		avert	adverse
nerd		sermon	
perm		cistern	
term		serene	
stern		sherpa	
fern		advert	
perch		serger	
terse		assert	
nerve		clergy	
verse		kerplunk	
serve		hermit	
berm		adverb	
germ		astern	

ow not followed by **n** or **l**

/ō/
owe
growth

plus -er
blower
lower
mower
grower
slower

/ou/
browse
dowry
tower
cower
power
dower
shower
flower
powder
chowder
dowdy
howdy

rowdy
vowel
bowel
cowel
towel
dowel
trowel
crowd
browser
dowse
zowie
coward
bowery

ow multisyllabic words

ow /ō/	**ow /ou/**
burrow	dowels
pillow	dowry
fallow	drowsy
disown	endowment
hallow	meow
window	powder
elbows	chowder
minnow	renown
escrow	towel
fellow	cower
follow	trowel
furrow	vowels
mellow	allow
narrow	browser
meadow	empower
bungalow	cowlick
shadow	however
willow	lowdown
arrow	eyebrows
bestow	waterfowl
billow	

/ch/ in multisyllabic words

whipstitched	pitchfork
bewitched	ratcheted
butterscotch	sketchbook
dispatched	sasquatch
birdwatchers	snitching
blotchy	switchback
catchphrase	overstretched
ditchdigger	switcheroo
etchings	thatched
flycatcher	topnotch
hatchback	uncatchable
hitchhiker	twitching
hopscotch	punching bag
ketchup	watchdog
kitchenette	poncho
kvetching	matchsticks
latchkey	nuthatch
benchmark	patchwork
blanching	witchcraft
entrenched	farfetched
goldfinches	homestretch
henchmen	munchkin
unquenchable	pitchman

-age /ij/

sewage	image	voltage
voyage	usage	salvage
average	damage	luggage
cabbage	mileage	coverage
cottage	manage	parentage
foliage	savage	Anchorage
overage	dosage	cartilage
plumage	verbiage	encourage
salvage	visage	hemorrhage
baggage	drainage	appendage
courage	marriage	scrimmage
footage	shortage	pilgrimage
message	poundage	percentage
package	blockage	freightage
portage	envisage	linkage
sausage	heritage	mortgage
selvage	language	wattage
village	beverage	spoilage
yardage	cribbage	suffrage
bandage	wreckage	patronage
leakage	carriage	voltage
passage	frontage	rummage
pillage	leverage	hostage
postage	advantage	garbage
storage	orphanage	brokerage
vintage	shrinkage	roughage

-age /äzh/

garage	triage
mirage	portage
corsage	sabotage
massage	decoupage
collage	camouflage
barrage	entourage
fuselage	
dressage	

-dge multisyllabic words

codger
widget
budget
gadget
midget
fidget
porridge
selvedge
partridge
cartridge
knowledge
acknowledge
hodgepodge

bludgeon
smidgeon
curmudgeon

-ange

/ā/	/ă/
angel	flange
range	orange
mange	phalange
change	
strange	
danger	/ă/ with **hard g**
ranger	anger
manger	banger
stranger	hanger
granger	
estrange	
exchange	
arrange	
derange	

soft g exceptions

**not soft g
(no e suffixes)**

girl
geese
gift
gizzard
get
gear
geisha
gecko
gibbon
giddy
gill
giggle
gilt
gilding
gingham
girder
girth
gird
gizmo
give
bagel
bogey
fogey
geek
hunger
geyser
mangel
giga
gild
gimp
argyle
ginkgo
gimlet
gimmick
gynecologist
gynecology
gelding
anger
tiger
begin
target
together
yogi

**soft g but not
before e, i or y**

veg
algae
margarine
fledgling
judgment
acknowledgment
abridgment

/j/ after a short vowel not -dge

college	**rigi: stiff or hard**	**frig: cold**
privilege	rigid	frigid
sacrilege	rigidity	frigidity
vestige	rigidify	refrigerant
allege	rigidness	refrigerator
magenta		refrigeration
magistrate	**reg, derivative of rect: to lead, to keep straight**	
agile		**vigi: watchful**
agitate		vigil
imagine		vigilant
fragile	register	vigilance
magi	registrant	vigilante
vegetable	regimen	
cogitate	regimental	
aboriginal	regimentation	
effigy		
religious	**digit: fingers or toes**	
prodigy		
indigenous	digit	
belligerent	digital	
pigeon	digitalis	
	digitalize	

/j/ after a short vowel not **-dge**

leg: law
legislate
legislator
legislation
legitimate

logic family: the art of speaking or reasoning
logic
illogical
illogically
logistics
logistical
logician
logicaster

logy: the study of
Such as : biology to biological to biologist

trag family: goat
tragic
tragedy
tragically
tragicomic
tragicomedy

magic: Latin and Old French
magic
magical
magically
magician

leg, lig, derivative of lect: to collect
legend
legendary
legible
illegible
intelligent
diligent

cent

**cent, centi
Latin: one hundred**

cent

percent

centigram

centigrade

centipede

centimeter

percentage

percentile

century

centurian

centennial

bicentennial

tricentennial

centr, centro, centri Greek: middle point, focal point

central

centric

concentrated

centricity

centrifugal

circumcenter

concentric

ecocentric

eccentric

egocentric

epicenter

geocentric

polycentric

ethnocentric

**cent, cant, chant
Latin: singing, a song**

accent

accentuate

accentual

incentive

disincentive

cantor

enchant

chanting

**scen, scan
Latin: to climb**

ascent

ascend

descent

condescend

escalate

scale

transcend

scandal

cide, cid, cise families

-cide, -cides, -cidal:
to kill, to cut down

biocide
pesticide
germicide
herbicide
cybercide
algicide
bovicide
fungicide
verbicide
genocide
infanticide
parenticide
homicide
suicide
patricide
matricide

-cise, -cis, -cide: to cut

cement
concise
decide
decision
decisive
incise
incision
precise
precision
precisionist
scissors
chisel
incisors

acid: sour, sharp

acid
acidity
acidic

rancid: spoiled, stinky

rancid
rancidness
rancidity

-cad, -cas, -cid: to fall

accident
coincide
cadence
cadaver
cascade
casual
decadence
decay
deciduous
incident
occasion
recidivism
chance
cheat
chute

ke/ki

keg	skee	kit	kismet	skit
key	skew	kin	kidnap	sky
Ken	skeet	kid	kidney	skid
keen	skewer	kip	kilter	skim
keel	sketch	kick	kindle	skin
keep	skelter	kind	kibble	skip
kelp	skedaddle	kill	kitten	ski
kept	skeleton	kiln	killjoy	skimp
kemp	skeptic	king	kindred	skiff
kennel	skein	kink	kinfolk	skill
kettle		kiss	kitschy	skirt
kerchief		kite	kickball	skivvies
kerplunk		kiddo	kitchen	skiffle
ketchup		kilo	kibitz	skirmish
kebob		kilt	kibosh	skitter
Kelvin		kitty	kidder	skiddoo
keno		kiwi	kilowatt	skillet
kernel			kimchee	skittle
Kevin			kimono	skinny
Keith			kindergarten	skipper
			kindling	

-ed /ed/ /id/

busted	responded
landed	avoided
acted	inspected
drifted	pretended
melted	defended
mended	extracted
granted	ingested
jointed	expected
sorted	ejected
needed	edited
ended	deducted
bonded	disrupted
twisted	exported
blasted	refunded
dented	unsanded
trusted	outlasted
painted	detracted
parted	mistrusted

-ed /d/

snowed	whispered
failed	happened
spilled	delayed
formed	sheltered
zoomed	showered
harmed	recalled
soiled	betrayed
stalled	enjoyed
toyed	rejoined
drained	ballooned
stayed	ordered
clanged	sharpened
stormed	installed
spooned	mastered
darned	decayed
drilled	flowered
seemed	replayed
coined	

ed /t/

jumped	impressed
picked	unthanked
milked	remarked
messed	backpacked
spooked	addressed
parked	scrapbooked
patched	picnicked
passed	relaxed
marched	impeached
stamped	unbrushed
stocked	trespassed
whisked	polished
tricked	padlocked
scuffed	handcuffed
stacked	discussed
marked	sandwiched
wished	outstretched
stomped	

mixed -ed

masked	unharmed
armed	gossiped
cooled	oppressed
pointed	entered
banked	employed
grunted	indented
dressed	reverted
trucked	embossed
swayed	galloped
belted	numbered
crusted	subtracted
scorned	refreshed
blended	established
peeked	focused
creeped	elected
chanted	uncharted
fainted	imprinted
cheered	unpublished
grafted	awaited
quilted	cornered
helped	maintained
banged	centered
spelled	whimpered

-ct /kt/ and -cked

pact	*an agreement*	packed
duct	*to lead*	ducked
tact	*to touch*	tacked
pict	*to paint*	picked
spect	*to look, see or watch*	specked
tract	*to pull*	tracked
flect	*to bend*	flecked
rect	*straight, or lead*	wrecked
flict	*to strike*	flicked
junct	*to join*	junked
punct	*point or to pierce*	punked
doct	*to teach*	docked
nect	*to join*	necked
coct	*to cook*	cocked
lict	*to leave*	licked
lact	*milk*	lacked
luct	*struggle*	lucked

/st/ and **/nd/**

past →	passed
mist →	missed
guest →	guessed
trust →	trussed
must →	mussed
bust →	bussed
mast →	massed
fest →	confessed

-nd	**-ned**
band →	banned
command →	manned
find	fined
mind	mined
bind	combined

words ending in **-id**

valid	putrid
timid	tepid
arid	hybrid
amid	liquid
candid	stupid
cupid	trepid
livid	morbid
humid	torrid
avid	rancid
lipid	acid
rapid	lucid
solid	rigid
florid	placid
pallid	druid
vivid	fluid
fervid	intrepid
rabid	pyramid
horrid	insipid
nitrid	orchid
cuspid	aphid

a /ə/ at the end of the word

data	drama	tundra
gala	villa	plasma
soda	ultra	asthma
nova	plaza	strata
lava	pizza	stigma
sofa	quota	contra
tuna	pasta	Bertha
coma	vista	tundra
puma	cobra	mantra
java	magma	stanza
yoga	panda	gotcha
aqua	scuba	hoopla
mica	tetra	zebra
tuba	fella	karma
hula	comma	llama
pica	libra	henna
okra	mamma	polka
diva	ninja	berka
china	larva	sherpa
saga	rumba	
cola	parka	
salsa	delta	
yucca	extra	

a /ə/ at the end of multisyllabic words

formula	arugula	Alaska
replica	banana	Alabama
grandma	gorilla	Oklahoma
grandpa	organza	Minnesota
persona	antenna	Nevada
stamina	portabella	California
vanilla	supernova	Indiana
bonanza	harmonica	Nebraska
algebra	ponderosa	Arizona
magenta	citronella	Florida
pajama	chinchilla	Georgia
granola	mozzarella	Montana
rotunda	vendetta	North Carolina
alfalfa	salmonella	North Dakota
spatula	propaganda	South Dakota
ricotta	bandanna	Pennsylvania
novella	rotunda	South Carolina
polenta	dilemma	West Virginia
umbrella	harmonica	Virginia
panorama	operetta	Iowa
Veronica	rutabaga	Louisiana
plethora	piranha	America
veranda	influenza	Canada

ai before n or l

gaily	Spain	plaintiff
attain	ordains	curtailed
domain	pertain	restraining
Bailey	dainty	romaine
retain	terrain	ascertain
details	ingrained	complaints
oxtail	trailer	available
derailed	acquainted	constraints
obtain	container	plantains
regain	detailed	refraining
retail	ailments	entertainment
sailor	bailouts	sustainability
Abigail	failure	rainforests
abstain	disdainful	tailgating
bailiff	moraine	maintaining
acquaint	sustaining	maintenance
cattail	tailors	fingernails
emailed	drainage	multigrains
saintly	entrails	parasails
availed	trainees	plaintively
braille	wainscot	semitrailer
prevail	migraine	remainders
contains	detainees	scatterbrained
explain	novocaine	trainability

ir / ər/

fir	smirk	perspiration
kir	swirl	giraffe
sir	whirl	thirtieth
irk	chirp	circumvent
bird	third	admiral
girl	mirth	aspirin
stir	squirm	birthday
dirt	circus	virtual
skirt	dirty	aspirate
shirt	sirloin	inspiration
firm	Irma	elixir
flirt	Irwin	miraculous
first	thirteen	irksomeness
birth	zircon	confirmed
birch	confirm	respirator
quirk	skirmish	nirvana
shirk	circuit	satirist
circa	circle	virtuous
twirl	squirrel	admirable
thirst	Shirley	thirteenth
squirt	virtue	infirmary
twirp	stirrup	recirculate

ai not before n, l

wait	braise	afraid
raid	waive	mermaid
waist	strait	maiden
braid	await	hollandaise
bait	daisy	mayonnaise
waif	waiver	appraise
praise	waiter	proclaim
claim	traitor	exclaim
gait	raisin	acclaim
plait		Band-aid
maim		gaiters
maize		paisley
raise		straight
aid		liaison
trait		parfait
staid		campaign
aim		chambermaid
faith		
traipse		
maid		
paid		

air words

air	fairy
lair	dairy
chair	mohair
hair	despair
fair	impair
flair	repair
pair	prairie
stair	affair
laird	hairdo
bairn	eclair
cairn	midair
	debonair
	airplane
	luminaire
	clairvoyant
	millionaire
	legionnaire

ai

/ĭ/
captain
bargain
chaplain
certain
curtain
fountain
villain
Great Britain
mountain
porcelain
portrait
chieftain

/ă/
plaid
daiquiri

/ī/
aisle
haiku
bonsai
daikon
Shanghai

/ĕ/
said
aforesaid
again
against

ay to ai
day → daily
pay → paid
lay → laid
say → said

v/v

me/ow	di/a/log	co/erce
suet	reliant	intuition
cruel	pliable	gradual
fuel	poetry	biography
client	reliable	variety
trial	diary	meteor
dual	reliant	diameter
dial	creative	meander
ruin	defiant	spontaneous
druid	truant	altruism
poet	piety	diabetic
liar	denial	genuine
giant	hideous	preamble
triumph	diagram	evaluate
bias	dialect	duality
poem	apnea	virtuous
cyan	diabolic	theater
	meteor	congruent
	museum	coexist
	deity	society

v/v, i /ē/

ra/di/o	pa/tri/ot	cham/pi/on
helium	audio	Columbia
trivial	caviar	Austria
oriole	zodiac	editorial
jovial	premium	material
mediate	patio	audience
podium	media	superior
menial	medium	tedious
sienna	period	pedestrian
alien	stadium	proverbial
lenient	piano	Olympiad
Juliet	idiom	barbarian
cardiac	studio	magnesium
obvious	chariot	ingredient
Indian	mania	bibliography
scorpion	folio	symposium
raffia	utopia	myriad
genial	phobia	gardenia
	Bolivia	amiable

long vowel in closed syllables

mold	both	enroll	pint
told		benzol	mild
sold	don't	mongol	child
scold	won't	patrol	wild
old		petrol	bind
bold	comb	creosol	find
cold		control	mind
fold	toll		wind
gold	droll		blind
hold	roll		grind
soldier	troll		hind
	stroll		kind
bolt	skoll		rind
colt			climb
dolt	host		
jolt	most		
molt	post		
volt	ghost		
holster			

ur

fur	furry	church	sandbur
urn	burly	burrow	surpass
yurt	curry	turban	urban
urge	hurt	Turkey	surname
surf	lurch	turnip	surplus
purl	slurp	bulgar	suburban
spur	nurse	burlap	survey
turn	purse	yogurt	turbine
curl	curse	burden	burger
slur	purge	burglar	curtsy
murk	surge	burrito	current
burp	burst	concur	murmur
curb	hurl	curfew	murrain
blur	gurgle	curtail	purpose
lurk	hurdle	curtain	pursuit
curd	purple	scurvy	sulphur
blurb	turtle	turmoil	surface
purrs	curdle	turnover	surgery
turf	turbo	unfurled	survive
blurt	absurd	jury	turnoff
burn	auburn	plural	turnkey
burnt	burden	perturb	topsey-turvey

-tion

verb	noun
abduct	abduction
edit	edition
delete	deletion
create	creation
erupt	eruption
ignite	ignition
adore	adoration
digest	digestion
pollute	pollution
violate	violation
admire	admiration
define	definition
produce	production
repeat	repetition
resolve	resolution
consume	consumption
orient	orientation
proclaim	proclamation
combine	combination
condense	condensation
reserve	reservation
consult	consultation

multisyllabic -tion

syllabication
reunification
fragmentation
encapsulation
deodorization
classification
triangulation
winterization
indoctrination
gentrification
detoxification
congratulation
automatization
volatilization
westernization
trivialization
thermalization
stigmatization
solidification
repolarization
prioritization
monopolization
legitimization
initialization
familiarization
exemplification
diversification
demystification
alphabetization
systematization
quadruplication
prognostication
personification
objectification
megacorporation
insubordination
externalization
revisualization
syllabification
precertification
hyperstimulation
editorialization
disqualification
circumnavigation
denaturalization
ultrafiltration
tintinnabulation
decriminalization
misrepresentation
intellectualization
conceptualization
institutionalization

-fle and **-ful**

rifle	helpful
trifle	mindful
stifle	stressful
ruffle	awful
piffle	hurtful
riffle	painful
sniffle	lawful
baffle	rightful
muffle	brimful
raffle	joyful
snuffle	spiteful
scuffle	forceful
shuffle	mouthful
truffle	youthful
waffle	dreadful
whiffle	scornful
	delightful
	neglectful
	suspenseful
	unsuccessful
	disrespectful

-ckle, -ickle, icle and ical /ikal/, /əkle/

buckle	icicle	comical	chemical
huckle	article	lexical	impractical
heckle	cuticle	medical	symmetrical
cackle	cubicle	topical	mechanical
crackle	vehicle	ethical	whimsical
freckle	follicle	logical	biological
speckle	particle	optical	ecological
spackle	clavicle	lyrical	historical
grackle	popsicle	radical	zoological
shackle	chronicle	typical	egotistical
chuckle	ventricle	cynical	evangelical
		magical	theatrical
fickle		musical	alphabetical
sickle		critical	astrological
pickle		mystical	geographical
tickle		tactical	mathematical
mickle		ironical	pathological
brickle		vertical	lackadaisical
prickle		tropical	
stickle		classical	
trickle			
strickle			

-ic

atomic	ethnic	agnostic
citric	toxic	bioethic
mimic	anemic	cosmetic
exotic	skeptic	dramatic
frolic	acrylic	logistic
heroic	hectic	pragmatic
ironic	bionic	alphabetic
cynic	fanatic	chocoholic
metric	nomadic	mosaic
public	angelic	nordic
rubric	aquatic	iconic
basic	caloric	diagnostic
septic	genetic	idealistic
fabric	lunatic	pathogenic
mystic	organic	supersonic
picnic	Pacific	Atlantic
gothic	cyclonic	academic

© 2019 Laughing Ogre Press®. All rights reserved.

-ic plus e, i, y suffixes

frolic
frolicked
frolicking
frolicky

panic
panicked
panicky
panicking

magic
magicked

mimic
mimicker
mimicked
mimicking

garlic
garlicky
garlicked

picnic
picnicking
picnicker
picnicked

traffic
trafficking
trafficker
trafficked

colic
colicky

plastic
plasticky

static
staticky

rollic
rollicking
rollicky
rollicked

doubling rule

run	rot	bet	wed
running	rotten	betting	wedding
wag	zip	nap	fit
wagged	zipper	napping	fitting
slur	top	let	nut
slurred	topped	letting	nutty
bud	red	star	fat
budding	redden	starry	fatten
hug	fur	dog	scar
hugging	furry	doggy	scarred
tar	jam	bag	rim
tarred	jammed	bagged	rimmed
dip	dig	pig	get
dipper	digging	pigged	getting
beg	mar	rip	jar
begging	marring	ripper	jarred
rub	tug	fog	wit
rubbed	tugged	foggy	witty
char	stir	gum	sip
charred	stirred	gummed	sipped
rap	mob	cap	spar
rapper	mobbed	capping	sparring
bar	fun	yum	blur
barred	funny	yummy	blurry

-ous, -us, -ess words

suffix -ous Latin, full of	-us not a suffix	suffix -ess Greek, female form
joyous	minus	lioness
bulbous	walrus	heiress
venomous	Venus	hostess
cankerous	bogus	tigress
ravenous	lotus	goddess
viperous	bonus	duchess
murmurous	virus	empress
cavernous	focus	actress
glutenous	rumpus	huntress
momentous	crocus	waitress
ponderous	hummus	mistress
sulfurous	humus	princess
blusterous	cactus	murderess
disastrous	stylus	sorceress
gluttonous	hiatus	temptress
plunderous	fungus	governess
carnivorous	circus	deaconess
boisterous	exodus	leopardess
complicitous	census	seamstress
coniferous	campus	
synonymous	versus	
	status	
	papyrus	
	cumulus	

-al plus -ly

totally	nationally
normally	politically
visually	technically
mentally	eternally
formally	criminally
naturally	diagonally
verbally	marginally
vocally	seasonally
brutally	viscerally
legally	bilaterally
digitally	electorally
equally	emotionally
legally	fraternally
morally	hexagonally
usually	medicinally
clinically	accidentally
fiscally	geothermally
globally	horizontally
manually	incidentally
centrally	ornamentally
generally	phonetically

-tle and -tal

usually a multisyllabic word	usually after a root or base -al Latin, like
title	vital
battle	fatal
rattle	metal
settle	petal
tattle	total
cattle	dental
gentle	portal
hurtle	brutal
bottle	mortal
kettle	postal
mantle	rental
beetle	mental
Myrtle	capital
nettle	orbital
chortle	pivotal
gruntle	coastal
shuttle	digital
scuttle	frontal
spittle	hospital
whittle	pedestal
startle	

words ending in -el /əl/

axel	duffel	tunnel
duel	enamel	weasel
fuel	dorsel	navel
cruel	funnel	channel
camel	hostel	counsel
angel	kennel	damsel
bagel	gospel	dreidel
bevel	morsel	falafel
dowel	nickel	flannel
easel	gravel	grapnel
gavel	laurel	strudel
bowel	kernel	mackerel
hazel	mantel	minstrel
jewel	marvel	sentinel
model	pummel	shrapnel
towel	sequel	mongrel
novel	mussel	pretzel
panel	pommel	quarrel
grovel	snivel	snorkel
revel	tassel	spaniel
level	swivel	tressel
libel	travel	pumpernickel
trowel		

ation / ative / able

relation→	relative→	relatable
fixation	fixative	fixable
education	educative	educable
formation	formative	formable
narration	narrative	narratable
operation	operative	operable
accusation	accusative	accusable
vegetation	vegetative	vegetable
regulation	regulative	regulable
consideration	considerative	considerable
imagination	imaginative	imaginable
application	applicative	applicable
separation	separative	separable
restoration	restorative	restorable
sedation	sedative	
decoration	decorative	
denomination	denominative	
generation	generative	
initiation	initiative	
renovation	renovative	
meditation	meditative	
indication	indicative	
innovation	innovative	

-ish

-ish in verbs of French origins	-ish Old English: like	-ish words that have developed not as a suffix ending
abolish	relish	
cherish	vanish	varnish
finish	British	outlandish
furnish	radish	
garnish	establish	
tarnish	Swedish	
impoverish	foolish	
anguish	sheepish	
flourish	Spanish	
embellish	childish	
lavish	boyish	
ravish	greenish	
demolish	ravish	
	girlish	
	reddish	
	selfish	
	mannish	
	diminish	
	finish	

elision and contractions

elision: deleting letters to shorten a word or a string of words without an apostrophe

monster	monstrous
wonder	wondrous
luster	lustrous
disaster	disastrous
tiger	tigress
number	numerous
do on	don
do off	doff
God be with you	goodbye
will I, nil I	willy, nilly
day's eye	daisy

contractions: deleting letters from a word or string of words to form shorter words with an apostrophe

madam	ma'am
must not	mustn't
of the clock	o'clock
it is	'tis
it was	'twas
you all	y'all
over	o'er

e rule dropping the **e**

grade	pollute
grading	polluting
prance	delete
prancing	deleted
bulge	infringe
bulged	infringing
horse	analyze
horsing	analyzing
craze	mistake
crazy	mistaken
solve	conspire
solving	conspiring
hype	exile
hyped	exiled
soothe	exchange
soothing	exchanging
taste	package
taster	packaging
cleanse	concentrate
cleansing	concentrating
change	continue
changing	continuing

e rule keep the **e**

sleeve	excite
sleeveless	excitement
hope	possessive
hopeful	possessiveness
tube	suspense
tubeless	suspenseful
spite	complete
spiteful	completely
sense	decisive
senseless	decisiveness
grace	remorse
graceful	remorseful
age	invisible
ageless	invisibleness
aware	advance
awareness	advancement
waste	purpose
wasteful	purposeful
ease	chastise
easement	chastisement

e rule exceptions

awful

wholly

duly

truth

fiery

ninth

truly

singeing

hingeing

bingeing

tingeing

dying

lying

hoeing

shoeing

canoeing

outrageous

courageous

gorgeous

advantageous

acreage

manageable

noticeable

serviceable

peaceable

pronounceable

knowledgeable

acknowledgeable

enforceable

marriageable

traceable

changeable

chargeable

judgment

argument

abridgment

doubling /e rule pairs

cars	parred	scrapped
careless	pared	scraped
stalling	spared	snippers
staleness	sparring	snipers
staring	mopped	slatted
starring	moping	slated
scarred	slimy	waded
scared	slimmer	wadding
malls	diner	gladly
males	dinner	glades
hers	stripped	bated
here's	striping	batty
barred	spineless	grimy
barely	spinning	grimly
balled	doled	sloped
baled	dolled	sloppy
taller	bidding	caper
tales	biding	capping

-cle plus -y

meaning full of, usually forming adjectives and adverbs

bubble	humble
bubbly	humbly
dimple	freckle
dimply	freckly
twinkle	cuddle
twinkly	cuddly
sniffle	jungle
sniffly	jungly
tingle	gentle
tingly	gently
marble	drizzle
marbly	drizzly
prickle	crinkle
prickly	crinkly
wobble	giggle
wobbly	giggly
noodle	sparkle
noodly	sparkly
wrinkle	bristle
wrinkly	bristly
ruffle	gristle
ruffly	gristly

multisyllabic **au /ȯ/**

implausible	daunted	gauntlet
sauna	staunch	caucus
paupers	hydraulic	defrauded
raucous	plausible	claustrophobic
fauna	somersault	auction
assaults	astronaut	marauding
baubles	augmentation	austere
audible	auburn	sauntered
autobiography	cauliflower	automatically
cauldron	exhaustive	caution
debauchery	gaudy	fraudulent
faucets	inaugural	tarpaulin
juggernaut	nautical	maundering
laudable	raunchy	holocaust
nauseate	sausages	mausoleum
traumatic	vaudeville	authorization
antiauxin	austerity	auditorium
cauterize	laundromat	unauthentic

sion /shən/

mit/ miss	stems ending in ss	stems ending in /d/
admit	cession	suspend
admission	session	suspension
	fission	
commit	passion	extend
commission	mission	extension
	scission	
submit		expand
submission	process	expansion
	procession	
permit		apprehend
permission	digress	apprehension
	digression	
omit		secede
omission	repress	secession
	repression	
remit		ascend
remission	express	ascension
	expression	
emit		comprehend
emission	possess	comprehension
	possession	
	confess	pension
	confession	tension
		mansion
	discuss	dimension
	discussion	

roots ending in **-ss**

press	to press
gress	to walk or step
fess	to talk, telling
cuss	to shake, strike, beat
cess	to be in motion, to yield
miss/mit	to send
sess	to sit, sitting

roots ending in -ss

press	**gress**	**fess**	**cuss**
depress	digress	confess	concuss
depressing	digressing	confessed	concussion
depressed	digressed	confessing	concussive
depression	egress	profess	discuss
impress	regress	profession	discussed
impressive	regressed	professed	discussing
impresses	regression	professional	percuss
impressible	congress	professor	percussion
suppress	congressional		repercussion
suppressive	transgress		
compress	transgressive		
compressed	aggressive		
compresses	regressive		
express	aggression		
expressing	digression		
expressive	transgression		
repress	progress		
represses	progression		
repressed	progressive		
oppress			
oppression			
acupressure			

roots ending in -ss

cess	**miss**	**sess**
abscess	remiss	assess
abscessed	dismiss	assessment
access	mission	assessable
accessed	admission	possess
accessible	omission	possesses
process	remission	obsess
processed	submission	obsessive
processional	emission	obsession
cessation	commission	repossess
cession	permission	session
concessive	emissary	
excess	missionary	
excessive	missile	
incessant	permissible	
necessary	promissory	
precession	submissive	
predecessor	transmission	
recess		
recessional		
secession		
secessionist		
success		
successful		

/shən/, /zhən/ exceptions

-shion

fashion

cushion

-xion

flexion

complexion

crucifixion

transfixion

fluxion

cion /zhən/shən/

coercion

suspicion

non-phonetic word

ocean

short e before -tion

discretion

short a before -tion

ration

national

y rule, change the y to i

envy	industry
envious	industrious
mercy	unhealthy
merciful	unhealthier
clumsy	embody
clumsily	embodied
fancy	dehumidify
fanciness	dehumidifier
cozy	inventory
cozier	inventoried
imply	mandatory
implied	mandatorily
heavy	gentlemanly
heavier	gentlemanliness
angry	debauchery
angrily	debaucheries
ready	disharmony
readied	disharmonious
deny	acceptability
denies	acceptabilities

y rule don't change the **y** to **i** with **i** suffixes

defy	understudy
defying	understudying
hobby	holiday
hobbyist	holidaying
okay	jockey
okaying	jockeying
fifty	canopy
fiftyish	canopying
bully	multiply
bullying	multiplying
gray	redeploy
grayish	redeploying
employ	accompany
employing	accompanying
display	gentrify
displaying	gentrifying
pity	dillydally
pitying	dillydallying
sashay	corduroy
sashaying	cordurorying
volley	essay
volleying	essayist
curtsy	photocopy
curtsying	photocopying

y rule don't change the **y** to **i** with vowel pairs

enjoy	destroy
enjoyed	destroyed
decoy	underpay
decoyed	underpayment
parlay	reemploy
parlayed	reemployed
mosey	portray
moseyed	portrayed
betray	convey
betrayer	conveyer
defray	doomsday
defrayable	doomsdayer

y rule when adding **s**, change the **y** to **i** add **es**

bunny	advocacy
bunnies	advocacies
jury	category
juries	categories
dairy	priority
dairies	priorities
agency	democracy
agencies	democracies
cavity	recovery
cavities	recoveries
galaxy	humanity
galaxies	humanities
refry	registry
refries	registries
imply	extremity
implies	extremities
artery	inequality
arteries	inequalities
comedy	climatology
comedies	climatologies

mixed endings rules

craze	mood	stuff
crazy	moody	stuffy
craziness	moodiness	stuffiness
fear	nerve	danger
fearful	nervous	dangerous
fearfully	nervously	dangerously
crab	slop	chum
crabby	sloppy	chummy
crabbier	sloppier	chummier
babe	six	laze
baby	sixty	lazy
babying	sixtyish	lazying
fog	sun	chat
foggy	sunny	chatty
foggiest	sunniest	chattiest
pup	dog	bud
puppy	doggy	buddy
puppies	doggies	buddies
manage	courage	outrage
manageable	courageous	outrageous
manageably	courageously	outrageously

ie

/ī/
lie
die
pie
tie

/īər/
fiery
plier
hierarchy

/ĕ/
friend
hygienic

/ear/
fierce
pierce
frontier
pier
tier
premier
cashier

/ĭ/
mischief
mischievous
sieve

/ē/
field
yield
wield
shield
chief
grief
brief
belief
thief
relief
chieftain
grieve
believe
achieve
aggrieve
reprieve
retrieval
relieve
fiend
diesel
besiege
hygiene
priest
spiel
shriek
niece
piece

ei

/ī/
feisty
heist
height
sleight (of hand)
fahrenheit
seismic

/ĭ/
counterfeit
forfeit
foreigner

/ĕ/
heifer

/air/
their
heir(ess)
heirloom

/ā/
rein
lei
vein
sheik
deign
feign
beige
feint
reign
skein
heinous
dreidel
geisha
lo mein
reindeer
surveillance
eight
weight
sleigh
freight
neighbor
inveigh

/ē/
weird
seized
leisure
caffeine
protein
codeine
neither
either
seizure
sheila

receive
conceive
deceive
perceive
deceit
receipt
conceited
ceiling

g not silent

magnet	magnitude
magnify	diagnostic
Agnes	prognosis
ignite	agnostic
ignition	magnum
ignore	sphagnum
stagnate	ignorance
magnolia	cognition
magnesium	incognito
dignity	ignoramus
cygnet	magnanimous
stagnant	

design	designation
	designate
	designee
	designator

resign	resignation

malign	malignant
	malignance
	malignity

indign (archaic word)	indignant
	undignified
	indignation

-gn

resign →	resignation
design	designation
malign	malignant
benign	benignant
impugn	impugnant
repugn	repugnant

arraign	arraignment
assign	assignment
align	alignment
realign	realignment

feign

deign

reign

oppugn

campaign

champagne

cologne

cu /ku/

cube	cued	concubine
cubic	cuticle	masculine
cute	occupy	articulate
Cuba	ridicule	persecute
cuke	vascular	incubate
cupid	cucumber	matriculate
vacuum	Hercules	documents
accuse	muscular	molecular
incubate	cumulus	ecumenical
macular	meticulous	electrocute
excuse	occupant	inoculate
recuse	cubical	meticulous
cubicle	acupressure	succulent
cumin	gesticulate	vernacular
circular	miniscule	masculinity
evacuate	acupuncture	inconspicuous
prosecute	speculation	acupuncturist
executed	binoculars	electrocuting
accuse	calculate	inconsecutive
miscue	barbecue	particularity
rescue	billiard cue	accusations
fescue	curlicue	ridiculousness
Cuban	porcupine	perpendicular

tu /choo/

ductule	intellectualize	estuary
contemptuous	tarantulas	virtually
factual	spatula	impetuous
accentuate	infatuate	mutually
spiritual	expostulate	statue
conceptual	capitulate	sumptuous
eventual	fistula	virtuoso
congratulate	actuaries	hyperintellectual
actual	effectually	misfortune
fortunate	fluctuate	presumptuous
gargantuan	constituent	postulant
tortuous	rituals	tumultuous
habitual	botulism	perpetually
impetuous	contextual	conceptualize
petulant	punctual	mutualization
conventual	instinctual	recapitulate
statute	mortuary	tempestuous
textual	obituary	intellectualizing
situation	contractual	sanctuaries
fatuous	pustule	capitulation

du /joo/

adulation	graduate
gradual	module
stridulate	acidulate
modular	dividual
pendulum	residual
arduous	glandular
fraudulent	demodulation
schedule	procedural
nodular	incredulous
assiduous	incredulity
education	undulate
glandule	individualize
credulous	decidual
deciduous	gradually

su, sure

/zhoo/	/zhər/	/shər/
usual	composure	pressure
casual	closure	assure
visual	foreclosure	ensure
casuist	incisure	insured
casuistical	leisure	licensure
	measure	tonsure
/shoo/	exposure	censure
issue	pleasure	reassures
consensual	treasure	coinsure
tissue	enclosure	acupressure
sensual	measurement	fissure

days of the week and months of the year

Sunday	January
Monday	February
Tuesday	March
Wednesday	April
Thursday	May
Friday	June
Saturday	July
	August
	September
	October
	November
	December

number words

one
first
eleven
eleventh

two
second
twelve
twelfth
twenty
twentieth

three
third
thirteen
thirteenth
thirty
thirtieth

four
fourth
fourteen
fourteenth
forty
fortieth

five
fifth
fifteen
fifteenth
fifty
fiftieth

six
sixth
sixteen
sixteenth
sixty
sixtieth

seven
seventh
seventeen
seventeenth
seventy
seventieth

eight
eighth
eighteen
eighteenth
eighty
eightieth

nine
ninth
nineteen
nineteenth
ninety
ninetieth

ten
tenth
hundred
hundredth

-logy/-logist

roots/prefix	meaning	-logy (study of)	-ist (person/job)
anthro-	mankind	anthropology	anthropologist
audio	sound	audiology	audiologist
biblio	book	bibliology	bibliologist
bio	life	biology	biologist
cardio	heart	cardiology	cardiologist
chrono	time	chronology	chronologist
cranio	head	craniology	craniologist
crypt	secret writing	cryptology	cryptologist
derm	skin	dermatology	dermatologist
etym	true meaning	etymology	etymologist
epi	among	epidemiology	epidemiologist
demio	people	epidemiologist	epidemiologist
geo	earth	geology	geologist
hemat	blood	hematology	hematologist
lexi	words	lexicology	lexicologist
myth	story	mythology	mythologist
nephro	kidney	nephrology	nephrologist
neuro	nerve	neurology	neurologist
onco	mass	oncology	oncologist
path	disease	pathology	pathologist
psycho	mind	psychology	psychologist
rhino	nose	rhinology	rhinologist
theo	divinity	theology	theologist
zoo	animals	zoology	zoologist

mixed -ct roots

abduction
overreact
contradict
bioelectrical
genuflected
fractionalization
dysfunctional
hectogram
directives
lactose
reluctantly
disconnection
indistinct
microstructures
activation
confectionary
detective
extinction
insecticides
perfunctory

circumspect
precinct
indoctrinate
semiconductors
imperfections
fluctuates
fructolysis
objectifying
preselected
nocturnal
picturesque
acupuncturist
introspective
chemotactically
aqueduct
fluctuating
electrocution
ineffectiveness
jurisdiction
malfunctioning
projectile

predictably
retroactive
concoctions
manufacturing
fictitiously
conflictingly
friction
thermojunction
relic
insurrection
octogenarian
rectangular
intersecting
restrictiveness
benefactors
circumspective
nocturnally
hectometers
rectification

y as /i/ with all syllable types

cycle	pyromaniac	dyslexia
lyceum	encyclopedia	pyromania
recycle	psychology	mystique
Phyllis	apocalypse	symposium
pylon	hysterical	psychiatry
thyroid	dysgraphia	gymnasium
Cyclops	hygienic	synagogue
gyroscope	hydraulic	Pennsylvania
myopic	encryptions	Polynesia
thymus	syndicate	synonymous
bicycle	physician	dysfunctional
cyanide	Odyssey	lymphatic
tricycle	synchronize	eucalyptus
syllable	sycamore	photosynthesis
mystery	hysterical	labyrinth
synopsis	synthetic	chrysalis
oxygen	abysmal	paralysis
nymph	olympian	symmetry
homonym	antonym	synonym

/y/ after **n** or **l**

billiard	minion
zillion	brilliant
junior	petunia
familiar	hellion
medallion	ammonia
senior	opinion
bunion	pneumonia
dominion	battalion
Daniel	civilian
begonia	dahlia
union	scallion
onion	companion
Spaniard	spaniel
pavillion	rebellion
regalia	galliard
scullion	vermillion
billion	peculiar
valiant	convenience
emollient	William
convenient	centillion

i /ē/

-ion
carrion
rampion
clarion
ganglion
champion
scorpion
criterion
campion
accordion
oblivion
centurion

-ian
guardian
circadian
obsidian
radian
median
meridian
Bohemian
Bostonian
Scandinavian
Austrian
Indian

-ious
odious
dubious
tedious
curious
devious
serious
previous
impervious
notorious
oblivious
fastidious
hilarious
laborious
insidious
nefarious
gregarious
precarious
illustrious

i /ē/

-ior
anterior
exterior
interior
inferior
ulterior
posterior
superior
excelsior

-iate
aviate
deviate
mediate
radiate
emaciated
herniate
alleviate
associate
enunciate
exfoliate
humiliate
abbreviate
ingratiate
circumstantiate

-ium
magnesium
ilium
odium
barium
helium
medium
calcium
premium
stadium
aquarium
condominium
solarium
gymnasium

-ient
ambient
obedient
expedient
gradient
nutrient
incipient
recipient
transient
subservient

i /ē/

-ial
imperial
pictorial
tutorial
janitorial
proverbial
trivial
axial
centennial
aerial
cranial
primordial
bacterial
menial

-iac
zodiac
celiac
maniac
cardiac
aphrodisiac
hemophiliac
hypochondriac
iliac
brainiac
insomniac
pyromaniac
kleptomaniac

-ience
ambience
audience
obedience
expedience
transience
subservience
experience

-io
portfolio
curio
radio
cardio
studio
patio
polio
ratio
barrio
scenario
pistachio
radicchio

i /ē/

-ia

mania

galleria

raffia

anemia

Bolivia

sangria

tilapia

academia

dyslexia

dysgraphia

dyscalculia

phobia

chia

gardenia

Maria

criteria

mafia

-ity

acid	civil
acidity	civility
cave	divine
cavity	divinity
unite	equal
unity	equality
sane	fatal
sanity	fatality
vane	human
vanity	humanity
agile	ideal
agility	ideality
breve	major
brevity	majority
dual	moral
duality	morality
grave	serene
gravity	serenity
obese	extreme
obesity	extremity
bovine	profane
bovinity	profanity
chaste	verbose
chastity	verbosity

-ine

/īn/, /ən/	/īn/	/ēn/
genuine	canine	marine
examine	bovine	benzine
heroine	divine	routine
imagine	feline	bromine
jasmine	iodine	chlorine
alkaline	columbine	cuisine
doctrine	porcine	latrine
gelatine	opine	machine
crinoline	alpine	sardine
determine	equine	dauphine
masculine	supine	figurine
intestine	carbine	gasoline
mandoline	stanine	morphine
margarine	turbine	nicotine
discipline	calamine	trampoline
urine	concubine	gabardine
engine	porcupine	grenadine
famine	valentine	limousine
medicine	strychnine	nectarine
lupine		tangerine
examine		quarantine
turbine		magazine
illumine		mezzanine
feminine		

ci /sh/

-al	-ous	-a
social	precious	acacia
financial	suspicious	Marcia
commercial	spacious	alopecia
facial	gracious	Leticia
special	ferocious	facia
official	vivacious	Alicia
artificial	precocious	Felicia
provincial	delicious	
glacial	vicious	
racial	luscious	
beneficial	atrocious	
especially	voracious	
antisocial	capricious	
prejudicial	malicious	
superficial	judicious	
	audacious	

ci /sh/

-an	-ent	ci /she/ with -ate
beautician	sufficient	appreciate
tactician	deficient	excruciate
esthetician	efficient	depreciate
arithmetician	proficient	officiate
logician	ancient	emaciated
magician	omniscient	dissociate
clinician		glaciate
mathematician		
mortician		
pediatrician		
optician		
diagnostician		
electrician		
musician		
politician		
physician		
statistician		
technician		
cosmetician		

ci /sh/

magician	glacial	audacious
auspicious	fiducial	capacious
loquacious	precious	facia
beautician	suspicious	hellacious
mortician	diagnostician	technician
commercial	beneficial	statistician
facial	delicious	judicial
optician	vicious	pugnacious
pediatrician	spacious	
clinician	gracious	
Marcia	financial	
cosmetician	politician	
voracious	ferocious	
capricious	acacia	
official	malicious	
sacrificial	multiracial	
provincial	judicious	
electrician	vivacious	
Leticia	musician	
lucious	antisocial	

s, ch, sch /sh/

s /sh/	ch /sh/	sch /sh/
sure	chef	schlep
censure	Chicago	schmaltz
insure	chaperone	schnauzer
ensure	chiffon	schmo
commensurate	Charlotte	schmuck
mensuration	charade	schnitzel
sugar	chivalry	schnook
sumac	parachute	schnozzle
tonsure	machine	schwa
	brochure	
	nonchalant	
	fuchsia	
	machete	
	pistachio	
	mustache	
	creche	
	niche	
	cache	
	quiche	
	panache	
	ruche	

ti /sh/

-al	**-ous**	**-an**
essential	cautious	Martian
potential	ambitious	Dalmatian
substantial	vexatious	Egyptian
partial	infectious	dietitian
residential	conscientious	gentian
spatial	superstitious	titian
influential	ostentatious	
confidential	repetitious	**-a**
existential	scrumptious	inertia
torrential	rambunctious	dementia
palatial	expeditious	militia
initial	flirtatious	minutia
experiential	nutritious	in absentia
impartial	pretentious	
martial	fictitious	**-ent**
referential	contentious	quotient
differential	fractious	patient
quintessential		
evidential		**-ence**
nuptial		patience

ti /sh/

ignition	Martian	torrential
prediction	dehydration	fascination
infectious	edition	fumigation
partial	consequential	gratification
coordination	differential	abolition
decongestion	juxtaposition	Dalmatian
implementation	legislation	rambunctious
fictitious	mineralization	militia
nutrition	dietitian	acceleration
Egyptian	palatalization	alphabetization
absentia	inertia	definition
superstitious	syllabication	electrocution
conversation	scrumptious	quantification
position	circumstantial	recreation
exhibition	Venetian	cannibalization
initial	influential	pretentious
cautious	martial	repetitious
ambitious	minutia	indoctrination
flirtatious	nuptial	obstruction
capitulation	presidential	variation
humiliation	benediction	confidential

Made in the USA
Monee, IL
21 July 2021